WHY HAVE A BAD DAY WHEN YOU CAN HAVE A GOOD DAY?

DR. HOWARD MURAD, M.D.

Wisdom Waters Press
1000 Wilshire Blvd., #1500
Los Angeles, CA 90017-2457

Quantity sales. Special discounts are available on quantity
purchases by corporations, associations, and others.
For details, contact the "Special Sales Department"
at the address above.

Printed in China

ISBN-10: 1939642205
ISBN-13: 978-1939642202

First Edition

17 16 15 14 13   10 9 8 7 6 5 4 3 2 1

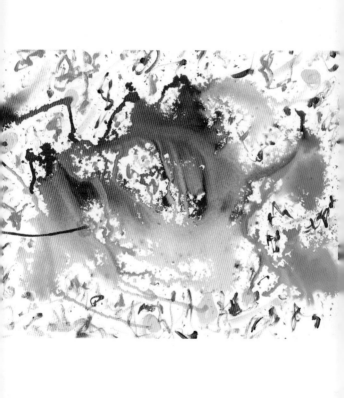

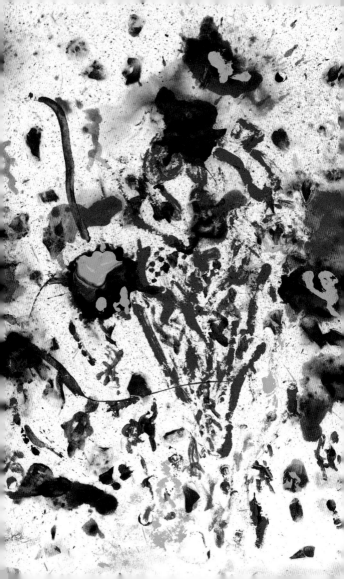

Everyone catches a few bad breaks every now and then, right? It's inevitable. But you don't have to give into them. Read this little book, and you'll discover that positive thinking can brighten the skies of even the rainiest day.

ABOUT THE ART

Self-expression is essential to human health and happiness. The author was reminded of that several years ago when he discovered a new outlet for his own irrepressible creative drive: painting. Interestingly enough, he's never taken any formal art classes, but his canvases are nonetheless sophisticated. His modernist style makes pure chance a key element in the artistic process. This results in explosions of color and form that expand the limits of imagination. Dr. Murad created the illustrations for this book hoping they would help you expand your imagination and envision a better tomorrow.

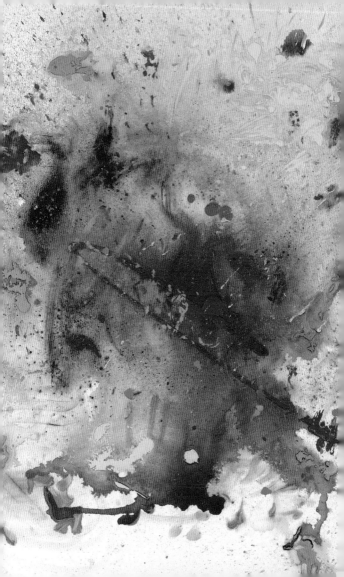

WHY HAVE A BAD DAY WHEN YOU CAN HAVE A GOOD DAY?

Perhaps you are having a bad day, and that's why you reached for this book when you saw the title *Why Have a Bad Day, When You Can Have a Good Day?* It's a question worth considering, and maybe you are asking yourself that question right now. I ask it myself often enough.

Everyone has a challenging day now and then, a day when nothing seems to go right. It's a wonder we don't have more of them since most of our days are chock full of problems and stresses. Our up-to-date and up-to-the moment way of life generates an enormous amount of what I often refer to as *cultural stress*. Clocks and computers rule our lives, and we want to answer every single phone message and respond to every one of the hundreds of emails we get each day. But we can't. There are so many demands made on us that we cannot possibly keep up with them all. This makes us feel like failures, like we're losing our grip. These negative feelings make us increasingly unhappy and unhealthy.

People feel better—and look much better, too—if they can avoid all this negativity. I encourage my patients to avoid negativity by introducing them to a whole new way of thinking. Several years ago, I began to compile a list of my insights into the nature of health and happiness. Often I share these with patients to help them take a fresh look at themselves and their lives. "Why have a bad day when you can have a good day?" is one of my insights, and in fact, it's the first one I actually wrote down. People really seem to take that one to heart. I do, too. But of course, like most people—doctors included—I don't always follow my own advice.

A while back, I was faced with a day like the one described above. I woke up in a bad mood or, as is sometimes said "on the wrong side of the bed," and from that point on my outlook grew steadily worse. My morning was a mess. Vital appointments got missed, essential papers got lost, and important phone messages went unanswered.

At 1:30 p.m. I was supposed to deliver a lecture on Inclusive Healthcare in Pasadena, but an appointment with a patient ran overtime and I got on the road much later

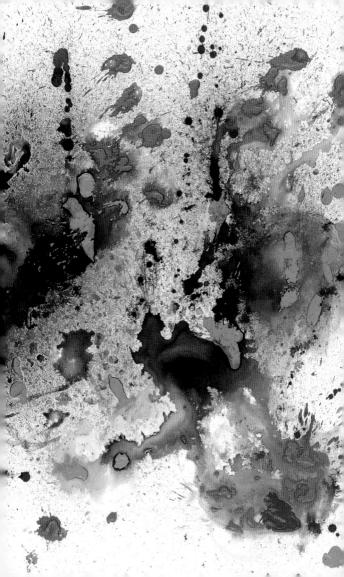

than expected. Pasadena is about an hour's drive from my office in Manhattan Beach, and it was obvious from the first that I was going to be late. The Los Angeles freeway traffic was even worse than usual and then I missed an exit. By the time I finally reached my destination and turned into the parking lot, my frustration level was peaking. How was I going to face the lecture audience and my hosts, the sponsors of this event, after showing up more than an hour late? This really had been an awful day—or so it seemed to me at the moment. Then, for some reason, my thoughts turned to a much earlier part of my life.

'My Left Leg Still Works'

Over the years, my personal journey has taken quite a few turns. I was born in Iraq in 1939. My family had lived there for many generations, but at that time the Middle East was changing even more rapidly than it is today. In 1946, when I was seven years old, we immigrated—fortunately to the United States. It was either leave when we did or never have a chance to leave at all. It was basically a matter of survival.

We came from relative wealth, and in Iraq we had a nice home with servants. My father was in the import/export business, and he did well, but all that changed quickly after we left Iraq. Within a year, my father was completely broke. At first we lived in a large house on Long Island with a big porch and lots of windows. But because of my father's financial difficulties, we ended up living in a 600-square-foot apartment in the New York City borough of Queens. We were a family of eight—a husband, wife, and six children (I was the youngest) crammed into a tiny apartment on an upper floor of a building with an elevator that never worked.

My father delivered messages in Manhattan for 75 cents an hour, which was then the minimum wage. Of course, there was no fax or email in those days, and he performed more or less that same function, carrying messages from one office to another in different parts of the city. That was a long fall for someone who had been a successful businessman. But my father was always a happy person, and despite his reversal of fortune, he never lost that quality.

Many years ago, I wrote a story about my father that appeared in *Reader's Digest*. It was a true story about the day my father was mugged in the subway on the way home from work. He was in his seventies at the time. Somebody took his money—he must have had a few dollars with him that day—beat him up, chipped his teeth, and broke his glasses. He barely managed to drag himself home and up the steps to our tiny apartment. My mother and the rest of us were frantic, because he really was in terrible shape. Even so, what he said to us was this: "Don't worry about it; my left leg still works."

No matter how desperate the situation, my father never failed to look at the positive side of things. I feel fortunate that he passed that attitude along to the rest of us. It helped me to see opportunities where others saw obstacles. It helped me to push past failures and not let them block the road to success.

On that day in Pasadena it would help me yet again. I remembered that terrible experience my father had so many years earlier. It occurred to me how trivial my own problems seemed compared to his, and I was reminded that in spite of all his pain and troubles he could still smile and joke

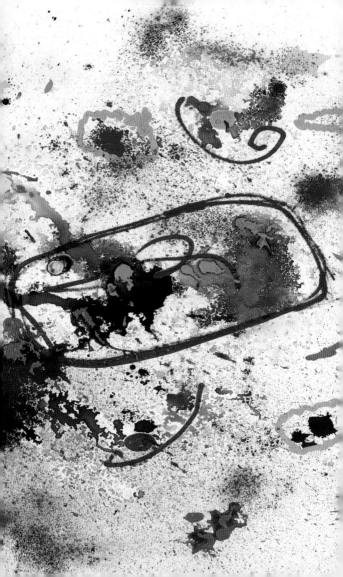

about what had happened. Perhaps, here in Pasadena I could do the same.   .

I gathered up my notes and hurried into what I fully expected to be an empty auditorium. In fact, some in the audience had understandably given up on me and gone on about their business. Much to my surprise, however, more than a few still patiently waited in their seats. Maybe they were the really committed ones, the people most excited about what I had to say, because I have rarely connected with a group of people the way I did that afternoon.

I told them about the difficult morning I had and how it reminded me of my father and what he had said after being mugged on the subway: "My left leg still works." They seemed to genuinely appreciate the story and they listened intently to what I had to say about Inclusive Health. I believe many of them were won over to this exciting new *inclusive* approach to healthcare. No doubt, this was one of my most productive speaking engagements, and I made a lot of wonderful new friends. As if by magic, a bad day had been transformed into a good one.

I believe that having a great day or a terrible day is less a matter of circumstances than it is of choice. You can choose to have a good day—or not. It's entirely up to you. This is the heart of my philosophy, and you should consider making it at least part of your own. Always try to focus on positive things instead of negative ones, and you'll be healthier and happier as a result.

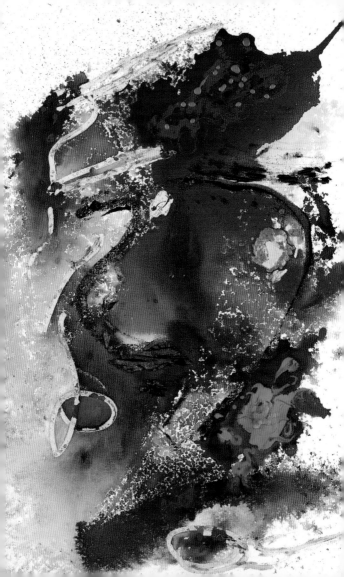

LIFE IS ART

One way to turn around a day that seems to be headed in the wrong direction is to open up your creativity. Set aside some time for art. It doesn't have to be painting, sculpture, or music—any sort of creative activity will do so long as you find it engaging. Likely, you'll discover that when you express yourself creatively, you'll feel better about your day, your surroundings, and yourself.

That's why I included the paintings you see in this book—to encourage you to make creative activities an everyday part of your life, just as I now make them part of mine. A few years ago a personal health crisis caused me to pick up a brush and try my hand at painting. I enjoyed the creative/artistic process far more than I ever thought possible. I truly believe that it helped me heal, and it certainly changed my perspective on life and medicine.

Since that time, I've incorporated art into my treatment programs and offered art therapy sessions at my spas and retreats. The results have been impressive. I am convinced that art therapy works, and study after study has shown this to be the case. For this reason, hospitals and clinics across America and the world are beginning to use art therapy to improve the emotional and physical health of their patients.

What art does for me and what I believe it does for my patients is reconnect us to an earlier time in our lives when play was completely free, when self-expression came easily, and when we didn't mind getting a little mud or paint on our hands and faces. Unfortunately, most of us begin to lose that sense of freedom and openness as early as the age of two. We are taught to conform, to behave properly, and follow the rules, in short, to color within the lines. We begin to believe that everything we do should be perfect, and since true perfection is impossible, we become frustrated and unhappy.

In my view, the most important thing to learn from art therapy is that there are no limits. Try not to get stuck painting within the lines. Better still, imagine that there are no lines.

As I hope you can see when you look at my paintings, I put no limits on art. When I paint, I make a few marks on a canvas, add some colors, and let a spray of water interact with them in a random way. Often this takes the canvas in a completely unexpected direction. How's it going to turn out? I don't know. All I want is to be surprised by the result. Sometimes, I am very happily surprised.

You can take this same approach to living your life. Be comfortable with yourself, and don't let your fear of failure hold you back. Once you learn that it's okay to paint outside the lines, your accomplishments will amaze you.

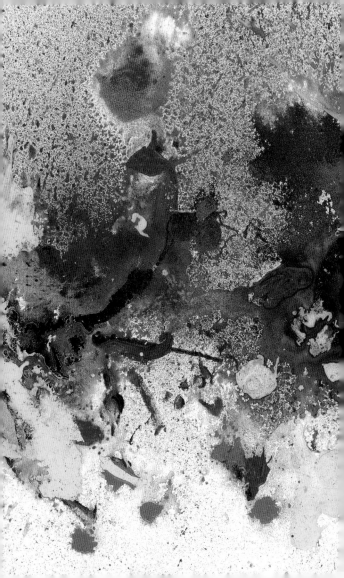

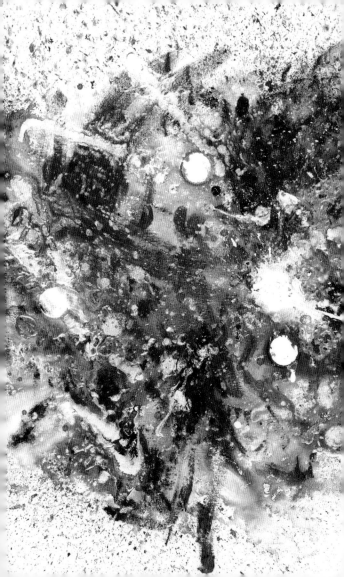

SIMPLE WORDS
OF WISDOM

Occasionally, I have what I believe to be a meaningful insight into the human quest for health and happiness. Usually these insights occur to me when I'm working with a patient or talking with a friend. Over the years I've collected hundreds of these insights, and I now think of them simply as my "sayings."

When patients visit my office to take part in our Inclusive Health program, I share several of these sayings with them. Many of the sayings are related in one way or another. They all have in common the idea that you can change your life for the better, that it's all a matter of how you approach the challenges of living. Here are a few insights that, in my way of thinking at least, are closely linked to the idea that any day can be a good day—it's just a question of perspective.

Smile daily, frown infrequently

When you smile, you're focusing on the positive, and when people see you smile, they're likely to believe you are a positive person. When you frown, the opposite is true. You're focused on negative things and likely to make a negative impression on others. Smile often and you just might find there are a lot of good reasons to keep smiling.

Don't focus on the minutia in life

You've heard the adage that "he can't see the forest for the trees." If you get too caught up in the details of life, you'll lose sight of the bigger, more important things. Keep in mind that success in almost any endeavor requires you to see the big picture and grasp the full sweep of events.

When your expectations are not met, see opportunity

Failure in one venture may lead to success in others. If you lose your job or don't get that raise you were expecting, you can complain or pout about it all you want, but it won't get you anywhere. Why not treat an apparent failure as an opportunity instead. Then, who knows where it may lead you? When engineering school didn't work out for me, I decided to go to pharmacy school. This led me into medicine, which turned out to have been the right field for me all along.

If it's not personal, don't take it personally

Our day-to-day lives are filled with stress—

traffic jams, long lines, emails, cell phone messages, and an endless swirl of things that demand our attention. This sort of cultural clutter often leads to a type of attention deficit disorder. We can only absorb sound bites. We read only a few lines at the beginning of a news article and we don't get the whole story. As a result, we get angry or anxious about things that are not really related to us in any way. We begin to take things personally that are not personal in any way.

Become free to be yourself

Trying to copy others won't help you become the person you were meant to be. What's wrong with being that genuine and capable person you really are? You have something unique to contribute. Celebrate yourself and what you have to offer.

Competency trumps genius

Competence often succeeds where genius, for one reason or another, may fail. You don't have to be a genius in order to succeed or to accomplish great things. You do need hard work, perseverance, and commitment.

Learn from your mistakes, don't project them on others

It's easy to complain about somebody else and, in this way, avoid taking responsibility for your own mistakes. That's a very destructive way of dealing with problems. You get no benefit from this and neither does anybody else. Instead of projecting responsibility on others, accept it yourself.

Success comes when you accept the possibility of failure

If you fail, just pick yourself up and try again. A single instance of failure—even a thousand such failures—need not spell

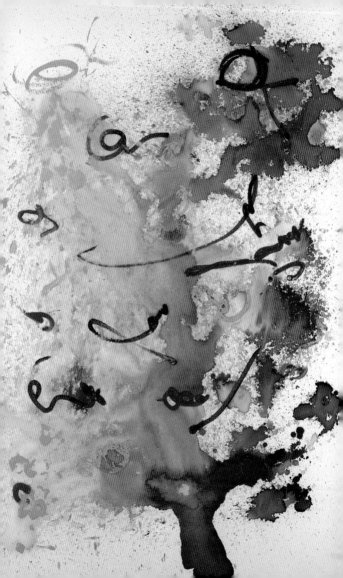

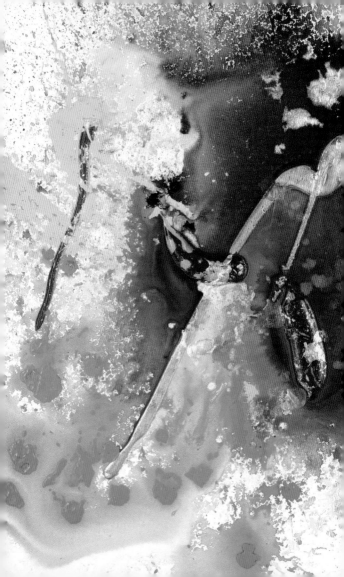

defeat. Don't be afraid of failure. Just keep on trying, because if you don't try, you'll never succeed.

The road to success runs through managing change

What's the most constant thing in life? It's change. You have to be able to manage that change if you want to be successful. If gas prices get too high, then maybe it's time to look for an alternative fuel.

Reduce complexity in your life

Complexity breeds stress and may be preventing you from reaching your goals. Simplify your daily life and you may discover that you are capable of far more than you ever thought possible.

Perfectionism leads to pessimism

We try to be perfect but, of course, this is the real world, and perfection is impossible.

When we strive for perfection we are bound to fail, and failure leads to pessimism because it makes us think we don't measure up, that we're not good enough to succeed. Naturally, you want to do things as well as you can, but strive for excellence, not perfection.

Healthy, hydrated cells are the key to ageless skin and a healthy body

Scientific research, including our own work with more than 4,000 individual patients, has shown a direct link between good health and high levels of cellular water. Basically, the more you increase your cellular water, the healthier you will become. The opposite is also true. When you lose cellular water, you open the door to aging and disease.

Healthy skin is a reflection of overall wellness

Healthy skin is not just a matter of appearances. Your skin is connected to every organ in your body. Generally speaking, when your skin looks good, chances are the rest of your body is basically healthy. Good skincare is also good healthcare.

Eat your water

You've probably heard you should drink eight glasses of water a day, but unfortunately, that won't do much to improve your health. If you drink that much water, it'll just run right through you without adding any of the critical moisture your cells need to survive. To properly hydrate your cells you need to eat raw fruits and vegetables. They contain lots of structural water that is slowly absorbed into the body. These same raw fruits and vegetables also contain healthful antioxidants and roughage to eliminate fat and help your body resist bone loss and cancer.

Before there was medicine there was food
If you ate well, you wouldn't need so much medicine. A major health concern in this society is our food, which is said to contain too many calories, too much fat, and too little real nutrition. I believe a far more important issue is how much—or how little—water is found in the foods we eat. Most of our food is too dry. It contains very little of the moisture required to keep our cells well hydrated and healthy. It is often said that people are overfed and undernourished. I say we're overfed and under hydrated.

Accommodate but don't let your life turn upside down

It's often necessary to accommodate others and take into consideration their needs and requests. However, you must never

carry the process of accommodation to the point that you lose sight of your own needs. Be your own person.

Real success is when you do what you are told you can't do

People measure success in many different ways. Some measure it by the size of the salary they earn or of the price of the car they drive. Others measure it by the amount of power, stock, or money they can accumulate. Still others measure it by winning in sports or other types of competition. But real success comes when you are able to accomplish what others believed was impossible. Even you may not be fully aware of your own hidden potential.

Turn the rest of your life into the best of your life

Your best years are still ahead of you. Even if that turns out not to be true, it sure helps to believe it. And I do believe it. There are always fresh adventures and wondrous new discoveries waiting for us out on the horizon. Embrace them, and you can be sure that the best is yet to come.

DR. HOWARD MURAD'S INCLUSIVE HEALTH APPROACH

A prominent Los Angeles physician, Dr. Howard Murad has successfully treated more than 50,000 patients. Drawing on his training as both a pharmacist and physician, he has developed a popular and highly effective line of skin care products that has won praise from health- and beauty-conscious people everywhere. A practitioner not just of medicine but of the philosophy of health, he has written dozens of books and articles, earning him a worldwide reputation as an authority on slowing the aging process.

Dr. Murad's approach to medicine is unique. It involves a concept he calls Inclusive Health. An alternative to traditional medical practice with its emphasis on the "spot treatment" of individual conditions or illnesses, the Inclusive Health approach treats the whole patient. Among other things, it considers the patient's diet, lifestyle, and emotional state as well as intercellular water—the hydration level of cells.

Years of painstaking research and experience with thousands of patients have shown Dr. Murad that human health and happiness are directly linked to the ability of cells to retain water. A poor diet and the stress of day-to-day living can damage the all-important membranes that form cell walls. Over time, the membranes become broken and porous, causing the cells to leak water and lose vitality. This, in turn, leads to accelerated aging and a wide variety of diseases and syndromes.

In his groundbreaking bestseller *The Water Secret*, published in 2010, Dr. Murad explained how to stop this process—and reverse it—through Inclusive Healthcare. This approach has three essential components. The first involves good skincare practices; the second, a healthy diet emphasizing raw fruits and vegetables; and the third, an overall reduction in stress combined with a more youthful and creative outlook on life.

The third component, which emphasizes our emotional state, may be the hardest part of the Inclusive Health treatment process for people to adopt. The breakneck pace of modern life with its freeways, computers, and cell phones, creates an enormous amount of what Dr. Murad describes as *cultural stress*.

To deal with this runaway stress, we live increasingly structured lives that are less and less open to the free play and creativity that make life worth living. *We can choose not to live this way.* But reducing stress and embracing a more youthful outlook often involves major shifts in lifestyle—changes in jobs, accommodations, locales, hobbies, habits, and relationships. It may even require a complete personal transformation of the sort sometimes identified with a single galvanizing moment of self-awareness. You may experience a transforming moment like that while walking on a beach, creating a work of art, driving through the countryside, or maybe just stretching your arms after a long night's sleep. Who can say?

To help his patients awaken to a better life, Dr. Murad has composed a substantial collection of personal insights or sayings that deliver bits of health advice, philosophy, and

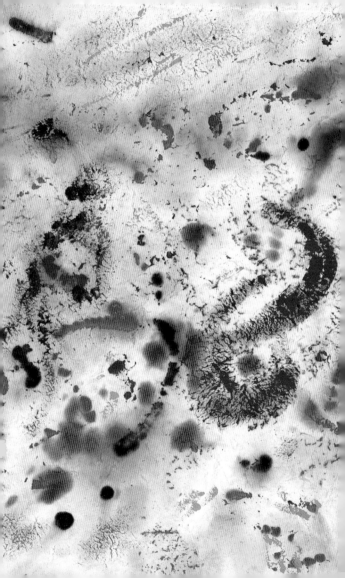

wisdom straight up, like strong coffee. In his medical practice, Dr. Murad shares these brief meditations with patients as a way of encouraging them to improve their health by adopting more youthful, creative, and health-conscious lifestyles. You may find them similarly inspirational. In addition to the insights you have already encountered in this book, here are a few others that you may find interesting and useful.

Learn from your mistakes.

Don't feel guilty for being yourself.

*Spontaneity leads to a more
fulfilling life.*

———————————

*Returning to your youth is the path
to happiness.*

———————————

*When going along the path of life,
always look up.*

———————————

*Make every day a vacation by
choosing a job and spouse you love.*

———————————

Beware of creating your own stress.

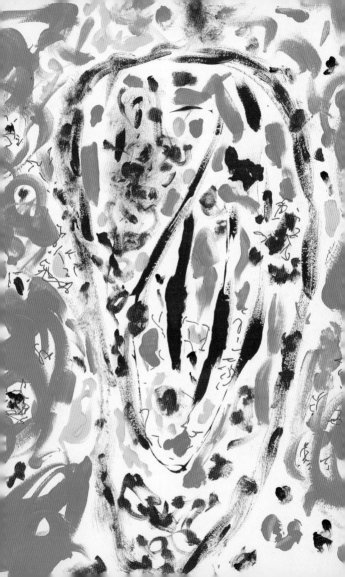

Don't be so hard on yourself.

———————————

Be thrilled with who you are.

———————————

*When you make your own journey,
you release others to do the same.*

———————————

Find your direction and focus on it.

———————————

*Look for what you can't find; it may
actually be in front of your eyes.*

———————————

*Look outside the box for solutions
to your problems.*

Accept the potential for the unexpected.

Success comes when you don't fear failure.

If it is no big deal, don't make a big deal about it.

To address life's ever-increasing, fast-paced changes, you need to be flexible.

The right answer is not always the right answer.

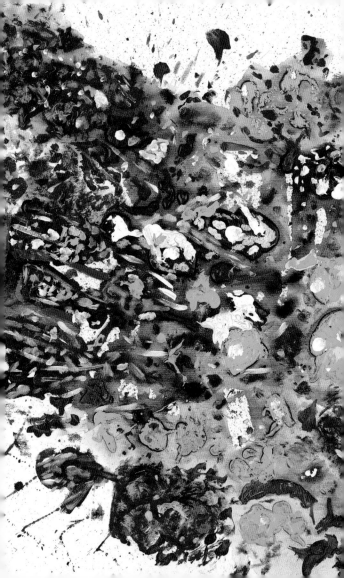

Dear reader,
Please share this book with others or give
it as a gift to family, friends, or business
associates. Also be sure to look for Dr.
Murad's other inspirational "little" books:

Give Yourself Permission to Be Happy

Be Imperfect—Live Longer

One Key Can Open Many Doors

Honor Yourself

The Best Is Yet to Come